Disappearing Acts

Toco Toucans
Bright Enough to Disappear

by Anastasia Suen

Consultants:

Dr. Glenn Tattersall
Brock University
St. Catharines, Ontario, Canada

Jerry Jennings
Emerald Forest Bird Gardens
Fallbrook, California

BEARPORT
PUBLISHING

NEW YORK, NEW YORK

Credits

Cover, © pablo_heman/Fotolia, and © Grafissimo/iStockphoto; TOC, © Christian Musat/Shutterstock, Dolnikov Denys/Shutterstock, and Eky Chan/Shutterstock; 4–5, © I. Schulz/Peter Arnold Inc.; 7, © Gail Shumway/Getty Images; 8, © imagebroker/Alamy; 9, © saragosa69/Shutterstock; 10, © SuperStock RF/SuperStock; 11, © Danita Delimont/Alamy; 12T, © Steve Bloom Images/Alamy; 12B, © Wildlife/Peter Arnold Inc.; 13, © Howard Buffett/Graint Heilman Photography; 15, © Kristen Gillet/SqueekPhoto.com; 16, © Gail Worth/Aves International; 17, Courtesy of the Blue-fronted Amazon Project 2007; 18, © Gail Worth/Aves International; 19, © Ade Johnson/EPA/Corbis; 20, © Gail Worth/Aves International; 21, © SA Team/Foto Natura/Minden Pictures; 22L, © Olga Gabay/Shutterstock; 22C, © Juniors Bildarchiv/Alamy; 22R, © Juniors Bildarchiv/Alamy; 22BKG, © Dolnikov Denys/Shutterstock, and Eky Chan/Shutterstock; 23TL, © Pablo H Caridad/Shutterstock; 23TR, Courtesy of the Blue-fronted Amazon Project 2007; 23CL, © I. Schulz/Peter Arnold Inc.; 23CR, © Dr. Morley Read/Shutterstock; 23B, © saragosa69/Shutterstock.

Publisher: Kenn Goin
Senior Editor: Lisa Wiseman
Creative Director: Spencer Brinker
Design: Kim Jones
Photo Researcher: Picture Perfect Professionals, LLC

Library of Congress Cataloging-in-Publication Data

Suen, Anastasia.
  Toco toucan : bright enough to disappear / by Anastasia Suen.
      p. cm. — (Disappearing acts)
  Includes bibliographical references and index.
  ISBN-13: 978-1-936087-45-7 (library binding)
  ISBN-10: 1-936087-45-6 (library binding)
  1. Toucans—Juvenile literature. 2. Protective coloration (Biology) —Juvenile literature. I. Title.
  QL696.P57S84 2010
  598.7'2—dc22
                              2009040370

For more information, write to Bearport Publishing Company, Inc., 101 Fifth Avenue, Suite 6R, New York, New York 10003. Printed in the United States of America in North Mankato, Minnesota.

112009
090309CGC

10 9 8 7 6 5 4 3 2 1

Contents

Look Again

In the lush tropical **rain forest**, brightly colored fruit can be seen growing in trees.

Look closely, however.

One of the pieces of fruit isn't really fruit.

It's a bird called a toco toucan!

The colors of a toco toucan act as **camouflage**, making the bird hard to see in the rain forest's colorful trees.

Hiding in Plain Sight

Toco toucans live mostly in trees in the rain forests of South America.

Their bright colors can trick other animals into thinking they are something they're not.

From a distance, the color and size of the toucan's red feathers, found under its tail, can look like a flower or a piece of fruit.

The color of the orange skin around the bird's eyes can also be mistaken for a flower or fruit growing in a tree.

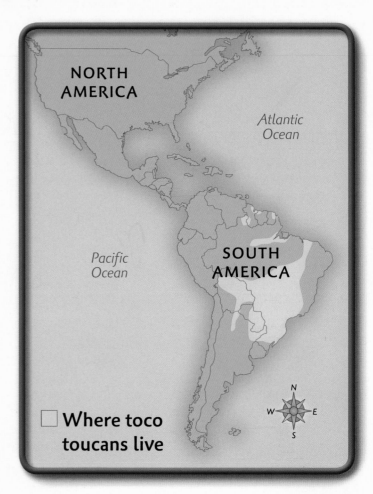

NORTH AMERICA

Atlantic Ocean

Pacific Ocean

SOUTH AMERICA

☐ Where toco toucans live

N
W E
S

The toco toucan's black and white feathers act as camouflage as well. They can be mistaken for shadows in the trees.

A Colorful Beak

The toucan's colorful **beak** also helps it blend into its surroundings.

The beak's red, yellow, orange, and black colors allow the toucan to be easily mistaken for a piece of fruit or a flower.

Animals that hunt the toco toucan, such as hawks, eagles, and owls, often fly right by the bird, never even seeing it.

Not including its beak, a full-grown toco toucan can be about 25 inches (64 cm) long. The bird's big beak can grow up to 7.5 inches (19 cm) long.

Time to Eat

The toucan also uses its big colorful beak to get food.

Sitting in a tree, the bird reaches with its beak to pluck fruit off branches.

The length of its beak allows the bird to reach for food that is not close by without moving its entire body.

Once the toucan has the fruit, it throws its head back and swallows.

In addition to fruit, toucans also eat insects and lizards, as well as other birds' eggs and **nestlings**.

tongue

A toco toucan has a featherlike tongue that is long and narrow. It is about the same length as the toucan's beak.

Hop and Glide

To get around the rain forest, a toucan hops from one nearby tree to another.

To get to trees that are farther away, the toucan flaps its wings a few times and then glides briefly over to them.

It grasps the branch with its claws when it lands.

Each claw has two toes that face forward and two toes that face backward for a tight grip.

toco toucan flapping its wings

toco toucan gliding

toes

Toco toucans spend most of their time in trees. They usually don't go down onto the forest floor.

Hidden in a Tree

At night, toucans sleep on tree branches.

They twist their necks so that their beaks rest on their backs.

Then they cover their beaks with their tail feathers and go to sleep.

The toco toucan sleeps in this position to keep its beak warm.

Eggs in a Nest

More than once a year, a female toucan lays up to four eggs in a nest.

The nests are found inside holes in trees made by other birds.

Both toucan parents take turns sitting on the eggs to keep them warm.

After 16 days, the eggs hatch.

toco toucans hatching

Toucan eggs are always white. They are hidden inside the tree, so they don't need to be camouflaged to stay safe.

Toucan Nestlings

When the nestlings hatch, they don't have feathers.

However, small bumps grow on their wings when the babies are two weeks old.

A feather will grow from each bump.

By the time the nestlings are about five weeks old, all of their black, white, and red feathers will have grown in.

After baby toucans hatch, their eyes don't open for three weeks.

Out of the Nest

Both male and female toucans take care of their babies.

For the first few weeks, the parents bring food to them.

After six to eight weeks, they teach the nestlings how to fly and find their own food.

Over the next few months, the babies' small, soft beaks grow longer and harder.

After several months, the babies will be as big as their parents and live their lives hidden in the trees.

a six-week-old toco toucan

Unlike other birds, male and female toucans look alike. Their feathers and beaks are the same color.

More Disappearing Acts

Toucans aren't the only birds that hide by looking just like the plants they live among. Here are three kinds of rain forest birds that are camouflaged with plant-like colors.

Parrots

Green Aracari

Parakeet

Glossary

beak (BEEK)
the hard, horn-shaped
part of a bird's mouth

nestlings
(NEST-lingz)
baby birds that
live in a nest

camouflage
(KAM-uh-flahzh)
colors and markings
on an animal's body
that help it blend in
with its surroundings

rain forest
(RAYN FOR-ist)
a large area
covered with trees
and plants where a
lot of rain falls

Index

Read More

Kite, Lorien. *Toucans.* Danbury, CT: Grolier Educational (1999).

McDonald, Mary Ann. *Toucans.* Chanhassen, MN: The Child's World (2006).

Learn More Online

To learn more about toucans, visit **www.bearportpublishing.com/DisappearingActs**

About the Author

Anastasia Suen has visited rain forests in Central America and Hawaii. The author of more than 100 books for children, she lives with her family in Plano, Texas.